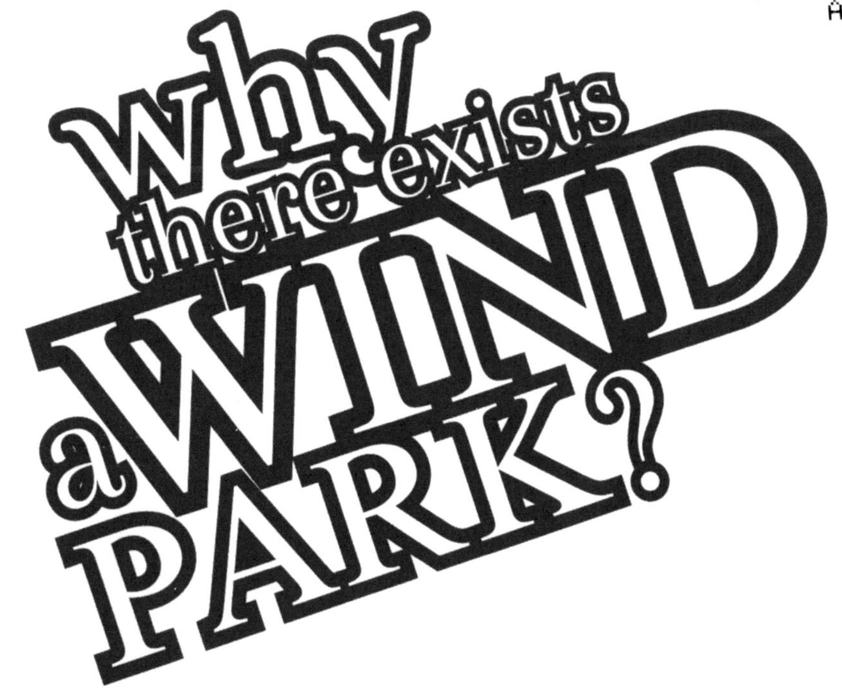

Series- *Children's Nature Quest*

Author

M Borhan

From

Big 6 Publishing

Pencil Sketch of a Wind Park

Wind parks play a crucial role in producing sustainable energy and decreasing reliance on non-renewable resources, thereby helping to alleviate the effects of climate change.

Biodiversity Preservation

Wind parks have a minimal ecological footprint, preserving biodiversity by avoiding habitat destruction and minimizing the impact on local flora and fauna.

Air Quality Improvement
By generating electricity without burning fossil fuels, wind parks reduce air pollution, improving overall air quality and protecting the health of ecosystems and wildlife.

Unlike some energy sources that require substantial water for cooling, wind parks contribute to water conservation, promoting the health of aquatic ecosystems and minimizing water usage.
Water Conservation

Climate
Change
Mitigation
Wind energy is a crucial tool in mitigating
climate change, helping to preserve natural
habitats by reducing the emissions that
contribute to global warming.

Erosion Prevention
Wind parks often involve careful land management, including measures to prevent soil erosion, maintaining the integrity of ecosystems and protecting against habitat degradation.

Noise Pollution Mitigation

Compared to some industrial activities, wind turbines produce relatively low levels of noise, minimizing disruption to wildlife habitats and promoting a more natural acoustic environment.

Wildlife Protection Measures
Responsible wind park planning includes measures to protect wildlife, such as bird-friendly designs and proper siting to avoid migratory routes and critical habitats.

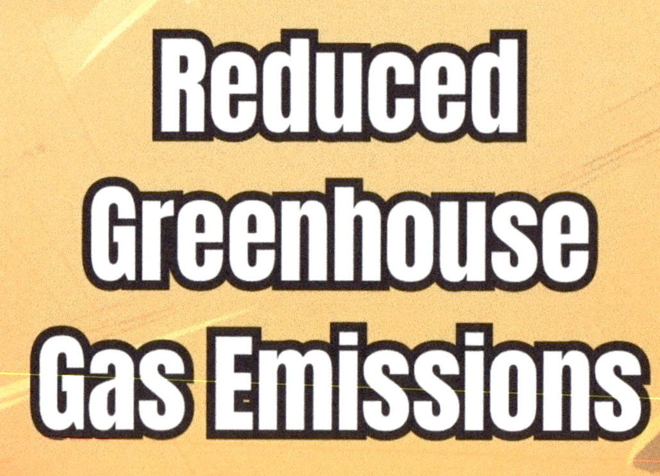

Wind energy's role in reducing greenhouse gas emissions directly benefits the natural environment by slowing climate change, preserving ecosystems that are sensitive to temperature shifts.

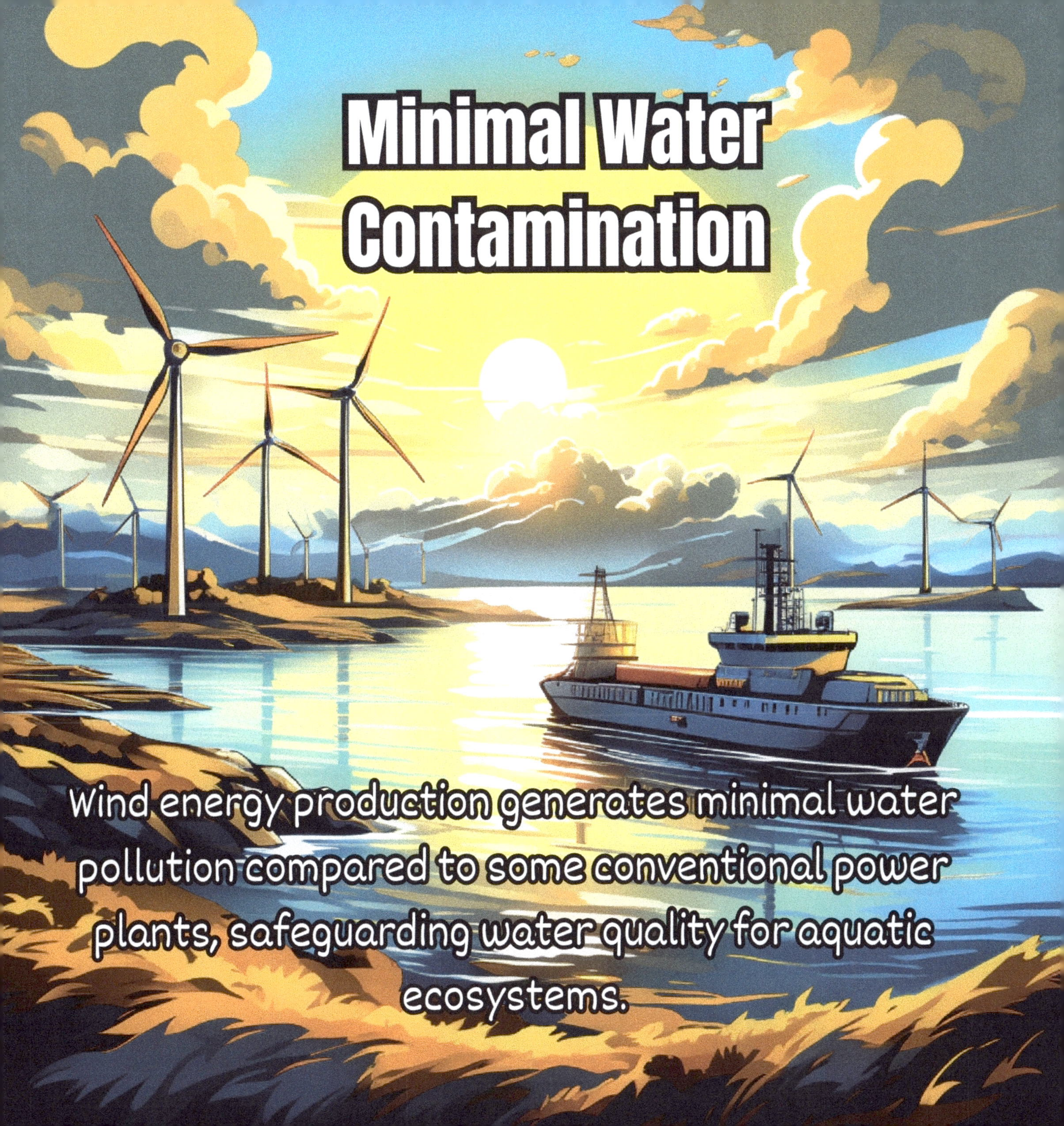
Minimal Water Contamination
Wind energy production generates minimal water pollution compared to some conventional power plants, safeguarding water quality for aquatic ecosystems.

Enhanced Ecosystem Resilience

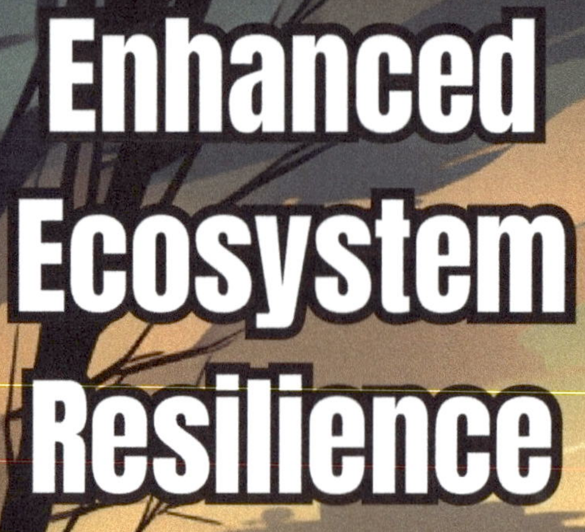

By promoting a shift away from environmentally harmful energy sources, wind parks contribute to the overall resilience of ecosystems, enabling them to better withstand environmental stressors.

Visual Impact
Mitigation
Wind parks are often designed to minimize visual
impact, ensuring that the natural beauty of
landscapes is preserved, benefiting both human
enjoyment and the health of local ecosystems.

Carbon Sequestration
Healthy ecosystems play a role in carbon sequestration, and wind parks, by reducing the need for carbon-intensive energy sources, indirectly support the preservation of natural carbon sinks.

Wind energy contributes to climate change adaptation by providing a sustainable energy source that helps ecosystems adapt to changing climate conditions.

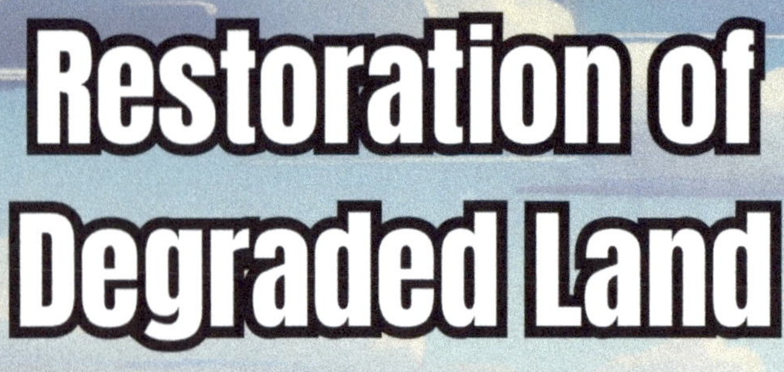

Wind park development can include the restoration of degraded land, bringing back biodiversity and ecosystem services to areas that may have been impacted by previous activities.

Pollution-Free Energy Generation
Wind energy production is pollution-free, ensuring that pollutants like sulfur dioxide and nitrogen oxides, which can harm ecosystems, are not released during electricity generation.

Promotion of Sustainable Practices
Wind parks exemplify sustainable energy practices, encouraging a broader shift toward environmental responsibility and fostering a culture of conservation.

Responsible Land Use Planning
Wind park projects often involve responsible land use planning, minimizing disruption to natural habitats and ecosystems.

Green Corridors

Wind park installations can create green corridors that connect fragmented habitats, promoting biodiversity by facilitating the movement of wildlife.

Educational Opportunities

Wind parks provide educational opportunities about renewable energy and conservation, fostering a deeper understanding and appreciation for nature and sustainability.

Long-Term Environmental Stewardship

The adoption of wind energy reflects a commitment to long-term environmental stewardship, safeguarding ecosystems for current and future generations.

www.ingramcontent.com/pod-product-compliance
Lightning Source LLC
LaVergne TN
LVHW072206150726
843469LV00056B/2288
* 9 7 8 9 8 4 3 5 6 1 0 3 9 *